The Lost Colony at Roanoke

ISBN-13: 978-0-15-360841-4
ISBN-10: 0-15-360841-2

4 5 6 7 8 9 10   805   13 12 11 10 09 08

Harcourt

SCHOOL PUBLISHERS

Visit *The Learning Site!* www.harcourtschool.com

The Age of Exploration

In the 1400s, many European nations were exploring the world. England, France, and Spain sent explorers around the world in search of new lands and new opportunities.

New Lands, New Opportunities

The rulers of these countries had many reasons for wanting to explore. New lands meant new opportunities to build colonies and expand their empires. These new lands also had resources, such as fur and gold, that were not available in Europe, or had been used up. Explorers often traded goods with the people they met.

Spain was the first nation during these times to send explorers to North America. In 1492, Christopher Columbus sailed from Spain and landed on an island in what we know as the Caribbean Sea.

Columbus and his crew sailed across the Atlantic Ocean in three ships.

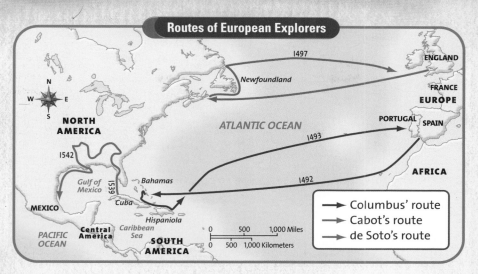

Routes of European Explorers

1497 · ENGLAND
Newfoundland
NORTH AMERICA
FRANCE
EUROPE
ATLANTIC OCEAN
PORTUGAL · SPAIN
1493
AFRICA
1542
1492
Gulf of Mexico
1539
Bahamas
MEXICO
Cuba
Hispaniola
PACIFIC OCEAN
Central America
Caribbean Sea
SOUTH AMERICA

0   500   1,000 Miles
0   500   1,000 Kilometers

→ Columbus' route
→ Cabot's route
→ de Soto's route

Explorers used many routes to get to North America.

Uncovering Secrets of the Land

Soon other countries sent explorers west to uncover the secrets of North America. In 1497, the king of England sent John Cabot to explore. The king of France also sent explorers to North America. Spain sent other explorers as well.

The rulers of these countries wanted to establish settlements in North America. They wanted to build colonies. People who lived in the colonies could send resources, such as lumber, gold, and sugar, to Europe.

Spain, France, and England all raced to establish colonies in North America. England's first attempt at permanent settlement of North America was on a little island off the coast of what we know as North Carolina.

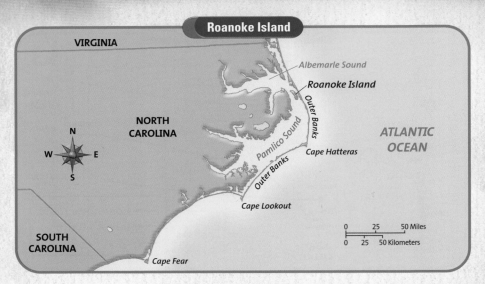

The explorers described Roanoke Island as "most pleasant."

The Exploration of Roanoke Island

In 1584, two ships left England for North America. These ships belonged to Sir Walter Raleigh. Raleigh had worked for Queen Elizabeth of England for many years before he organized the expedition to North America.

Raleigh did not lead the explorers aboard the two ships, however. The explorers were led by Captain Arthur Barlowe. They weighed anchor off the coast of North Carolina on July 13, 1584, and set out for the shore.

From their landing place, the explorers went south. They reached some high dunes and climbed them. From the top of the dunes, they saw water on both sides of the land. They realized that they were on a barrier island, one of a line of long, narrow islands that stretched along the coast.

Explorers and Indians Meet

Four days after they landed, the explorers met a group of American Indians of the Roanoke tribe. The two groups spent a short time trading. Then some of the explorers went by boat to nearby Roanoke Island.

Roanoke Island had dense woods and diverse plantlife. The explorers saw that fish, game animals, and birds were plentiful. At the north end of the island was a Roanoke village. The tribe welcomed the explorers.

When the ships returned to England, two Roanoke named Wanchese and Manteo went with them. Captain Barlowe gave Raleigh a glowing report of Roanoke Island. It was chosen as the site of England's first colony in North America.

John White's watercolor painting of an American Indian village

The First Colony, 1585–1586

In the spring of 1585, Sir Walter Raleigh sent seven ships from England to Roanoke with a total of 108 people. Wanchese and Manteo returned with them.

On June 26, the ships reached North America. The crew explored the islands along the coast for a month. Finally, on July 27, the people disembarked on Roanoke Island.

Building Begins

Ralph Lane was made governor of the new colony. The colonists built a fort at the north end of Roanoke Island. They built their houses nearby.

The American Indians planted crops and made fish traps for the English settlers. Instead of expressing their appreciation, however, the English treated the Roanoke harshly. The American Indians became angry with the settlers and stopped helping them. By June of 1586, the settlers and the Roanoke were fighting.

The colonists were ex[pecting] ships from England. Whe[n they] failed to arrive, they grew desperate. Just in time, word came that help was near. A fleet led by Sir Francis Drake was off the coast.

Sir Francis Drake

Governor Lane asked Drake for help. Drake gave him two choices. If the settlers chose to stay at Roanoke, he would give them a ship of their own, with supplies and sailors. The second choice was to return to England with him. At first, Lane accepted the offer of a ship for the colony. Lane changed his mind, however, after a storm blew it out to sea. When Drake sailed for England, all the settlers went with him.

The Colony Is Abandoned

When the delayed supply ships arrived at Roanoke, they found the colony abandoned. Sir Richard Grenville,

the commander of the fleet, left 15 crew members behind with enough food to last for two years. Grenville wanted to make sure that England would keep its claim on the new land until more settlers arrived.

Sir Francis Drake sailed in a ship such as the one pictured.

The Lost Colony, 1587

Sir Walter Raleigh still wanted to establish a colony in North America. In 1587, he decided to try again. Raleigh organized a group of 150 colonists, including women and children. He promised 500 or more acres of land to every settler willing to go.

Based on the original explorers' report, Raleigh selected a different site for the new colony. He told the new settlers to make their home in the Chesapeake Bay area. This area had a better port than Roanoke Island had.

The colonists left England in three ships on May 8. Some had been members of the first Roanoke colony.

Raleigh wanted the colonists to settle around Chesapeake Bay, farther north than Roanoke Island.

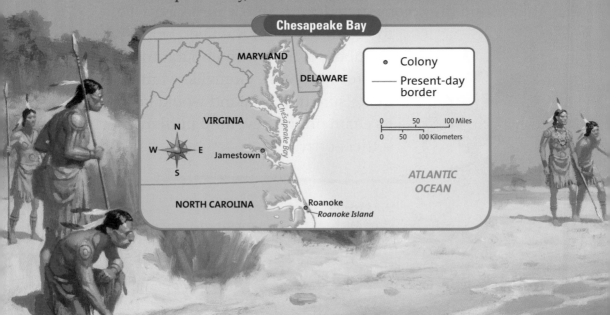

Chesapeake Bay

MARYLAND

DELAWARE

- Colony
- —— Present-day border

VIRGINIA

N W E S

Jamestown

0   50   100 Miles
0   50   100 Kilometers

ATLANTIC OCEAN

NORTH CAROLINA

Roanoke
Roanoke Island

Chesapeake Bay

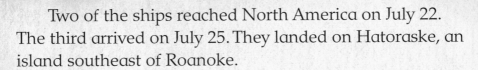

Two of the ships reached North America on July 22. The third arrived on July 25. They landed on Hatoraske, an island southeast of Roanoke.

John White, who had been chosen governor of the colony, led a group to Roanoke. They wanted to meet with the men Grenville had left there in 1586. They only found the bones of one man. There was no sign of the 14 others.

The next day, White and his party trekked to the site of the fort. It had been completely destroyed, yet many of the houses still stood. Against Raleigh's orders, the colonists did not go on to Chesapeake Bay. They decided to settle at the original site on Roanoke Island. They repaired the houses that were still standing and built new ones.

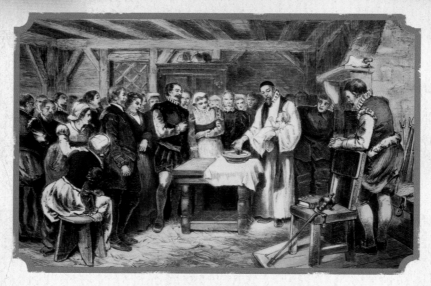

Virgina Dare was the first baby born to English parents in North America.

Troubled Times

The Roanoke were hostile toward the new settlers. They were still bitter about the harsh treatment by the first colonists. One settler was killed soon after the landing.

Help came from Manteo, one of the two American Indians who had gone to England in 1584. While there, Manteo had learned to speak English. He had relatives on nearby Croatoan Island. Through his efforts, the Croatoan tribe became friendly toward the settlers.

The Croatoan told Governor White that it was the Roanoke who had killed Grenville's 15 men. White decided to take revenge. On August 8, he attacked the Roanoke village.

The attack was a horrible mistake. The Roanoke had been warned and had already fled. The people White attacked were friendly Croatoan who had come to the village to look for food left behind by the Roanoke.

Again, Manteo came to the settlers' aid. He convinced the Croatoan that the attack had been made in error. They agreed to forgive the settlers. As a reward for his services, the English gave Manteo the name Lord of Roanoke.

The Birth of Virgina Dare

Governor White's daughter Eleanor and her husband, Ananias Dare, were among the settlers. On August 18, 1587, she gave birth to a daughter. She and her husband named the baby Virginia, after the Virginia territory. Virginia Dare was the first child of English parents born in North America.

This marker at Fort Raleigh commemorates the birth of Virginia Dare.

The Missing Years

Soon the settlers' supplies ran low. Governor White returned to England in 1587 to bring back more supplies and more colonists.

Before White left, the settlers discussed moving to the mainland. If they did need to leave the island before White returned, they agreed to leave him a message.

Colonists at Roanoke Are Abandoned

However, White was unable to return to Roanoke for three years. While the colonists were in North America, war had broken out between England and Spain. Ships full of supplies for the colonists were turned over to the English navy. They were needed for fighting Spain's great fleet, called the Armada.

In 1588, two small ships were able to sail to North America. The ships were attacked by the French navy, and their supplies were stolen. The ships were forced to return to England without ever reaching North America.

The Spanish Armada

St. Augustine, Florida, was a Spanish colony.

England defeated the Spanish Armada in 1588, but the war with Spain went on for a few more years. Spain wanted to destroy England's colony in North America. The Spanish sent a ship to find the colony. Near Roanoke Island, the Spanish found a harbor. They saw signs that the English had been there, but they did not find any people.

Governer White Organizes Rescue Ships

In the meantime, Governor White had tried to organize a fleet of ships to bring supplies and new settlers to the Roanoke colony, but his plan failed. With the help of Sir Walter Raleigh, White was able to travel to North America on a fleet headed for the West Indies. He was unable to take with him any supplies or settlers, however.

The ships sailed from England on March 20, 1590, and spent months sailing in the West Indies. On August 15, 1590, they anchored off Hatoraske Island.

The Mystery of Roanoke

From the ship, Governor White could see smoke rising from Roanoke Island. He hoped this meant that the colonists were still alive. A small party set out for Roanoke.

The party tried to reach Roanoke again on August 17. One boat capsized in the dangerous waters. Despite this accident, the party set out in two boats.

The next morning, the men landed on Roanoke. They walked toward the site where the settlers had been. The houses had been taken down. A wall of tree trunks enclosed the area. The word CROATOAN was carved into one post.

The landing parties returned to their ships. They planned to go to Croatoan the next day. However, a sudden storm prevented them. They gave up and returned to England.

FORT RALEIGH NATIONAL HISTORIC SITE

The Lost Colony site is now part of the National Park Service. In the museum, visitors can see objects found at the site. In 1937, the site held a performance of a play titled The Lost Colony. The play has been presented every summer since then.

The Colonists Remain Lost

Governor White did not have the money to make another voyage. By 1593, White had given up hope of finding the colonists.

Many historians believe that the colonists moved inland. They may have joined friendly American Indian tribes. Some believe that they were killed by hostile tribes. Some think that Spain attacked the colony as it had planned.

In 1607, England founded its first permanent colony in North America in present-day Virginia. The settlement was named Jamestown in honor of King James I of England.

The Jamestown colonists knew about the Lost Colony. Many tried to learn where the settlers had gone. Local American Indians reported that they had seen Europeans living in various places. The colonists hoped the American Indians could tell them more, but no facts ever came to light. No Lost Colonists were ever found.

Think and Respond

1. What was the Lost Colony?

2. What caused problems between the settlers and the American Indians?

3. What prevented Governor White from returning to Roanoke?

4. Why did England want to have a colony in North America?

5. Do you think it is important to find out why the Lost Colony disappeared, or should it remain a mystery? Why?

 # Activity

With three or four of your classmates, role-play members of the Lost Colony talking together after Governor White returned to England. Act out a conversation in which the colonists discuss the colony's problems and what they should do about them. End the conversation by arriving at a decision about what to do.